Mysteries of the Sea

Mysteries *of* the Sea

How Divers Explore the Ocean Depths

By Marianne Morrison

NATIONAL GEOGRAPHIC

WASHINGTON D.C.

One of the world's largest nonprofit scientific and educational organizations, the National Geographic Society was founded in 1888 "for the increase and diffusion of geographic knowledge." Fulfilling this mission, the Society educates and inspires millions every day through its magazines, books, television programs, videos, maps and atlases, research grants, the National Geographic Bee, teacher workshops, and innovative classroom materials. The Society is supported through membership dues, charitable gifts, and income from the sale of its educational products. This support is vital to National Geographic's mission to increase global understanding and promote conservation of our planet through exploration, research, and education.

For more information, please call
1-800-NGS-LINE (647-5463) or write to the following address:
National Geographic Society
1145 17th Street N.W.
Washington, D.C. 20036-4688
U.S.A.

For information about special discounts for bulk purchases, please contact
National Geographic Books Special Sales at ngspecsales@ngs.org

Visit the Society's Web site: www.nationalgeographic.com

Copyright © 2006 National Geographic Society

Text revised from *Divers of the Deep Sea* in the National Geographic Windows on Literacy program from National Geographic School Publishing, © 2002 National Geographic Society

All rights reserved. Reproduction of the whole or any part of the contents without written permission from the publisher is prohibited.

Published by National Geographic Society. Washington, D.C. 20036

Design by Project Design Company

Printed in the United States

Library of Congress Cataloging-in-Publication Data

Morrison, Marianne.
  Mysteries of the sea : how divers explore the ocean depths / by Marianne Morrison.
    p. cm. -- (National Geographic science chapters)
  Includes bibliographical references and index.
  ISBN-13: 978-0-7922-5954-1 (library binding)
  ISBN-10: 0-7922-5954-8 (library binding)
  1. Underwater exploration. 2. Deep diving. I. Title. II. Series.
  GC65.M65 2006
  551.46--dc22

                    2006016323

Photo Credits
Front Cover: © Darryl Torckler/ Stone/ Getty Images; Spine: © Georgette Douwma/ Digital Vision/ Getty Images; Endpaper: © Georgette Douwma/ Digital Vision/ Getty Images; 2-3: © Emory Kristof/ National Geographic Image Collection; 6: © Getty Images; 10: © Emory Kristof/ National Geographic Image Collection; 13 (bottom): © Hulton Archive/ Getty Images; 14: © Bates Littlhales/ National Geographic Image Collection; 15: © Luis Marden/ National Geographic Image Collection; 16: © NOAA; 17: © Darlyne Murowski/ National Geographic Image Collection; 18-19, 19 (bottom): © NOAA; 21 (top): © Al Giddings Images; 21 (bottom): © Wolcott Henry/ National Geographic Image Collection; 22: © Wildlife Conservation Society; 24: © William Beebe/ National Geographic Image Collection; 25: © Peter David/ Taxi/ Getty Images; 26: © Getty Images; 28, 29, 30: © NOAA; 31: © Ralph White/ Corbis; 33 (top): © Woods Hole Institute; 33 (left): Emory Kristof/ National Geographic Image Collection; 33 (right): © APL/ Corbis; 8-9: Illustrations by Levent Efe, CMI; All Other Illustrations by Dimitrios Prokopis.

Contents

We know little about many of the amazing creatures that live beneath the sea.

The Oceans

People have explored most of the land on Earth. They've climbed the highest mountains, hiked the deepest forests, and traveled to both Poles. But if you think we've explored most of Earth, think again.

Earth is covered by about three times more water than land. And most of that water has never been explored. We know a lot about the surface, or top, of the ocean. But what lies below the surface?

Arctic Ocean

Atlantic Ocean

Pacific Ocean

Indian Ocean

The Four Zones of the Ocean

The ocean is divided into four zones. The amount of light and the depth of the water change from zone to zone.

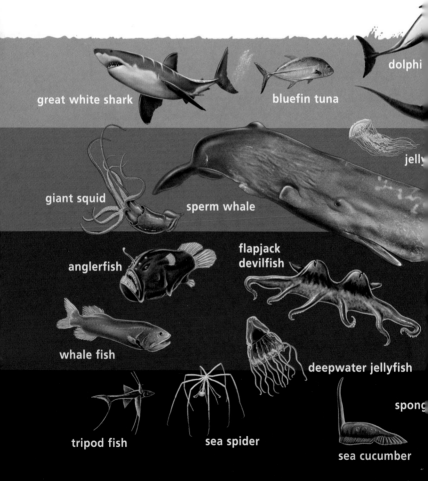

dolphi

great white shark

bluefin tuna

jelly

giant squid

sperm whale

flapjack
devilfish

anglerfish

whale fish

deepwater jellyfish

spong

tripod fish

sea spider

sea cucumber

Note: Creatures and zones are not drawn to scale

sea turtle

sea horse

manta

The Sunlight Zone is near the ocean's surface. It receives the most light and has the most plants and animals.

orange roughy

hatchetfish

In the Twilight Zone, the light is very dim. At this depth, it is darker and colder. There are not as many plants and animals.

siphonophore

gulper eel

angler shrimp larvae

In the Midnight Zone, there is no light. It is completely dark and very cold. Strange creatures live at this depth.

The Trench Zone is the deepest part of the ocean. The deepest part of this zone is almost 7 miles (11 km) deep.

abyssobrotula

Chapter 1

Divers Go Deeper

The Diving Helmet

People have always wanted to explore below the surface of the ocean. The earliest divers held their breath and went as deep as they could go before needing more air. That wasn't very deep.

Then the diving helmet was invented in 1839. It was copper and very heavy. The helmet was attached to a heavy diving suit. An air hose from the surface brought air to the diver. A diver could go 230 feet (70 m) below the surface wearing a diving helmet.

A Navy diver suits up for a dive in 1914.

Place: Aegean Sea, off the coast of Greece
Date: May 1869

It takes 30 minutes for the diver to put on his diving gear. The heavy helmet is finally bolted to his suit. The air hose is attached. Weights are put on his chest and his back. His boots also have lead weights on the bottoms.

The diver is helped into the water. The weights help him sink. Air pumps into his helmet as he goes down.

He looks through the faceplate in his helmet. A parrotfish swims up to get a better look at him. A school of squid seems to hang in the water.

Finally, he is 230 feet (70 m) below the surface. A ray rises from the sandy bottom. The diver starts to walk slowly towards the rocky ledge where sponges grow. He begins to collect the sponges that he will sell.

◀ Divers collect sponges like these from the ocean floor.

▼ A diver wearing a diving helmet and heavy suit prepares to dive.

The Aqua-Lung

Divers could go deeper with the diving helmet, but it did not allow them to move around freely. They dreamed of swimming like fish. In 1943, Jacques Cousteau made this dream come true. He invented the

Jacques Cousteau prepares to dive. Divers have gone as deep as 210 feet (64 m) using the Aqua-Lung.

Aqua-Lung. This tank allowed the diver to breathe air and move about freely underwater. It was the start of scuba diving. Scuba stands for "self-contained underwater breathing apparatus."

Beneath the Sea

Diver: Jacques Cousteau
Place: Mediterranean Sea, off the coast of France
Date: June 1943

Cousteau straps the heavy tanks of air on his back. He puts on his diving mask and fins. With 50 pounds (23 kg) on his back, he waddles into the sea.

He looks down and sees a canyon far below. He kicks his fins and starts down. He glides through the water like a fish. Then he lets the air out of his lungs. He watches the bubbles rise. Next he takes a deep breath. It works! He can breathe underwater.

Cousteau's dream has come true. He can swim freely. There are no ropes, hoses, or heavy helmet to slow him down. He rolls over. He does a somersault. He even stands upside down on one finger.

Using the Aqua-Lung enables a diver to swim with the fishes.

A diver wearing a Jim suit is lowered to the ocean floor.

The Jim Suit

Divers wanted to go much deeper and still be able to move around freely. This was a problem. The deeper you go, the colder it gets. You start to feel as if you are being crushed because of water pressure. Water pressure is the weight of water. The more water above you, the more weight presses on you.

The Jim suit was invented to let divers roam freely in very deep water. It is named for the first man who used it, Jim Jarratt. The Jim suit is a heavy metal suit. It looks like a spacesuit. It protects the diver from the cold and the water pressure.

Odd fish, such as these hatchetfish, live deep within the ocean.

This metal diving suit was used in 1937 to explore a shipwreck. Its use led to the creation of the Jim suit.

Attached to the Jim suit's arms are two metal claws for lifting things. Inside, the diver can breathe air that is cleaned and recycled. For most dives in the Jim suit, the diver is lowered on a rope from the surface.

Some Jim suits
have thrusters
that help the diver
move around.

Beneath the Sea

Diver: **Sylvia Earle**
Place: **Pacific Ocean, off the coast of Hawaii**
Date: **October 19, 1979**

Everything around her is blue as she begins her dive. Earle is strapped to a small submarine. As she goes deeper, the water changes from blue to gray and finally black. She feels a soft thump as the submarine touches the bottom.

Finally, they stop at 1,250 feet (381 m). The pilot releases the strap holding her onto the submarine. She is free to explore the deep.

A small circle of light from the sub shows an amazing and wonderful world. A dozen bright red crabs with long legs sway on a red sea fan. A lantern fish swims by with lights glowing on its side. Earle looks away from the light and sees sparks of living light. Tiny fish light up as they brush against her. She explores strange coral that glows in the dark.

After two and a half hours on the ocean floor, Earle heads back to the surface.

Sylvia Earle dove 1,250 feet (381 m) in a Jim suit strapped to a small submarine.

A red sea fan sways on the ocean floor.

William Beebe sits on top of his invention, the bathysphere.

Chapter 2

Diving Ships Go Deeper

The Bathysphere

Parts of the ocean are almost 7 miles (11 km) deep. People needed to invent diving ships in order to dive that deep. To make these deep dives possible, William Beebe and Otis Barton invented the bathysphere.

This strange round chamber on a wire cable was like an elevator to the deep. It could go up and down, but it couldn't move sideways. The bathysphere looked like a giant eye. The divers inside recorded every animal that passed before its round window, or porthole.

Beebe and Barton were the first to enter that zone of the ocean where there is no light at all. Only the light from a small bulb inside the bathysphere helped them see the amazing things of the Midnight Zone.

William Beebe and Otis Barton dove 3,028 feet (924 m) in the bathysphere.

Beneath the Sea

Diver: William Beebe and Otis Barton
Place: Atlantic Ocean, off the coast of Bermuda
Date: August 15, 1934

Beebe squeezes head first through the small opening to get inside. Once inside he makes room for Barton. There's not much room. They untangle their legs and get ready. Then the heavy door is bolted shut.

They begin to go down. The deeper they go, the darker it gets. It also gets colder, much colder. Then they start to see the strange creatures of the deep. An anglerfish swims by. As they go deeper, several hatchetfish swim through the beam of light from their little light bulb.

Finally, they enter the Midnight Zone of the ocean. This is a world of complete and total darkness. They reach a depth of 3,028 feet (924 m). They stay there for only three minutes. They have just enough air for the trip to the surface.

Anglerfish live in the Midnight Zone.

The Bathyscaph

To help divers go even deeper, a diving ship called a bathyscaph was invented. It could move up and down but could not move around easily.

In 1960, Jacques Piccard and Don Walsh used a bathyscaph named the *Trieste* to dive almost 7 miles (11 km) down. They explored the Trench Zone, the deepest known part of the ocean.

No person has ever returned to this depth. These two men still hold the record for the deepest dive.

Jacques Piccard and Don Walsh dove to the bottom of the ocean in the *Trieste.*

Beneath the Sea

Diver: **Jacques Piccard and Don Walsh**
Place: **Pacific Ocean, off the coast of Guam**
Date: **January 23, 1960**

Huge waves pound the *Trieste* as Piccard and Walsh climb on board. Then, at 8:23 in the morning, they begin their dive. Three hours later they are 27,000 feet (8,235 m) deep and still going down. They go deeper and deeper.

As they near the bottom, fear comes over them. What if the ocean bottom is a thick ooze? The ship could get stuck. No one could save them. They would freeze to death in this cold, black world.

Finally, they reach the bottom. They do not get stuck. They are 35,800 feet (10,919 m) deep. This is almost 7 miles (11 km) down. Piccard looks out. He sees a flatfish with two round eyes swimming away. Life exists this deep!

They spend only 20 minutes on the bottom before they begin to go up. After more than eight and half hours, the dive is over. They reach the surface again.

Submersibles

A submersible is like a small submarine. Once in the water, a submersible can move around. It also has lights that help divers see underwater. An explorer can stay underwater in it for about ten hours.

Today, divers use many different machines to explore the deep. Some submersibles have robots attached to them. The crew inside the submersible can send the robot into small places to take pictures.

A moray eel swims next to a reef.

Submersibles like this one allow divers to explore underwater for long periods of time.

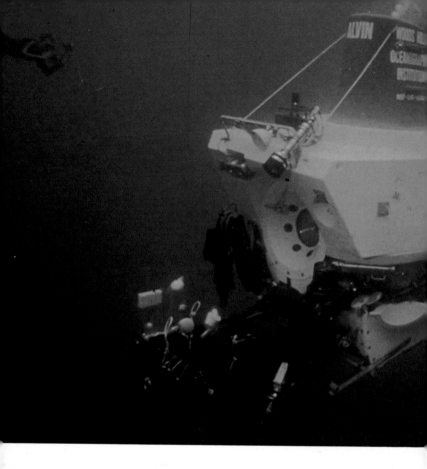

In 1986, Robert Ballard led a team to
explore the *Titanic*. This famous ship sank
in 1912 and was over 2 miles (3 km) deep
when found. Ballard went down in the
submersible named *Alvin*. Attached to *Alvin*
was the robot named *Jason Junior*, or *JJ*.

This submersible named *Alvin* dove 12,460 feet (3,800 m) to explore the *Titanic*.

A robotic arm retrieves a leaded glass window from the shipwrecked *Titanic*.

Beneath the Sea

Diver: **Robert Ballard**
Place: **Atlantic Ocean, off the coast of Newfoundland**
Date: **July 1, 1986**

It takes more than two hours to get down to the *Titanic*. This is the third dive to the *Titanic* in the little submersible *Alvin*. But this is the first time Ballard and his team will use the robot *JJ* to explore the inside of the ship.

They reach the deck of the ship. Slowly they steer *Alvin* inside. They go down the main staircase of the ship. Then they park *Alvin* and send *JJ* out into the ship. They guide the robot down into the ship. They see the grand clock on the landing of the staircase. Then they see a beautiful light hanging from the ceiling by its cord.

The team makes ten more dives after this one. They see an amazing collection of things from the ship. They see the dinner plates, beds, sinks, bathtubs, doorknobs, and windows that were once part of this great ship. They are the first explorers to find and explore this famous sunken ship.

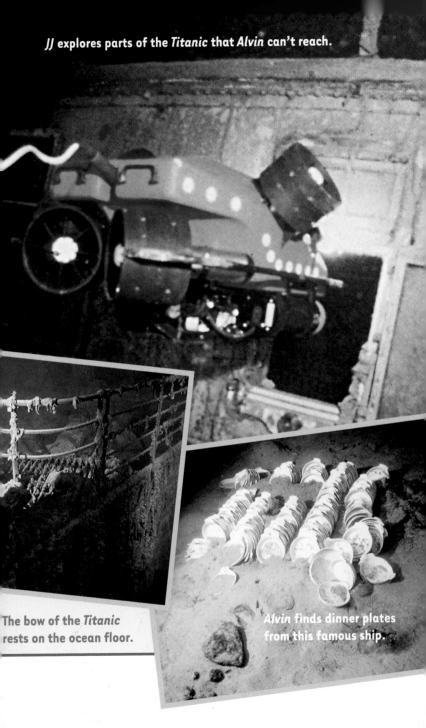

JJ explores parts of the *Titanic* that *Alvin* can't reach.

The bow of the *Titanic* rests on the ocean floor.

Alvin finds dinner plates from this famous ship.

A History of Deep Sea Dives

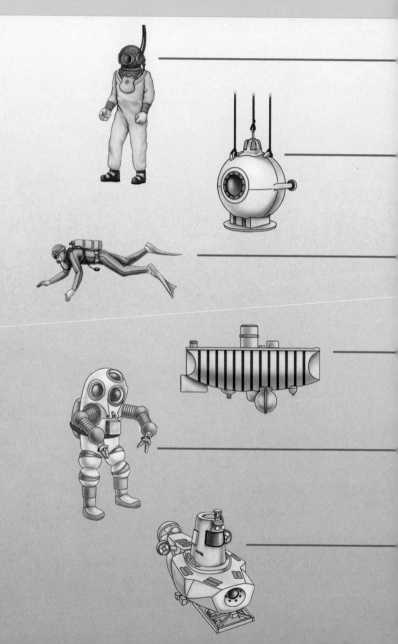

Diving Helmet:
230 feet (70 m). Augustus Siebe invented the closed diving helmet in 1839.

Bathysphere:
3,028 feet (924 m). William Beebe and Otis Barton reach the Midnight Zone in 1934.

Aqua-Lung:
210 feet (64 m). Jacques Cousteau makes the first dive with an Aqua-Lung in 1943.

Bathyscaph:
35,800 feet (10,919 m). Jacques Piccard and Don Walsh reach ocean bottom in 1960.

Jim Suit:
1,250 feet (381 m). Sylvia Earle completes the deepest solo dive in a Jim suit in 1979.

Submersible:
12,460 feet (3,800 m). Robert Ballard explores the *Titanic* using *Alvin* in 1986.

How to Write an A+ Report

1. Choose a topic.
- Find something that interests you.
- Make sure it is not too big or too small.

2. Find sources.
- Ask your librarian for help.
- Use many different sources: books, magazine articles, and websites.

3. Gather information.
- Take notes. Write down the big ideas and interesting details.
- Use your own words.

4. Organize information.
- Sort your notes into groups that make sense.

- Make an outline. Put your groups of notes in the order you want to write your report.

5. Write your report.

- Write an introduction that tells what the report is about.

- Use your outline and notes as you write to make sure you say everything you want to say in the order you want to say it.

- Write an ending that tells about your report.

- Write a title.

6. Revise and edit your report.

- Read your report to make sure it makes sense.

- Read it again to check spelling, punctuation, and grammar.

7. Hand in your report!

Glossary

Aqua-Lung   an underwater breathing machine that enables a diver to swim freely

bathyscaph   a diving ship designed for deep-sea exploration

bathysphere   a round diving ship that could only go straight up and down

depth   how deep something is in the water

diving helmet   copper helmet with an air hose that brings fresh air from the surface to the diver

Jim suit   self-contained, deep water diving suit for a single diver

recycled   to be reused

submersible   a small underwater craft used for deep-sea research

water pressure   the weight of water

Further Reading

• Books •

Earle, Sylvia A. *Dive! My Adventures in the Deep Frontier.* Washington, DC: National Geographic Society, 1999. Ages 9-12, 64 pages.

Earle, Sylvia A. *National Geographic Atlas of the Ocean: The Deep Frontier.* Washington, DC: National Geographic Society, 2001. Adult, 192 pages.

Matsen, Brad. *The Incredible Record Setting Deep-Sea Dive of the Bathysphere.* Berkeley Heights, NJ: Enslow Publishers, 2004. Ages 10-14, 48 pages.

Matsen, Brad. *The Incredible Quest to Find the Titanic.* Berkeley Heights, NJ: Enslow Publishers, 2003. Ages 10-14, 48 pages.

Submarine (Eyewitness Books). New York, NY: DK Children, 2003. Ages 9-12, 64 pages.

• Websites •

British Broadcasting Company
http://www.bbc.co.uk/nature/blueplanet/blue/master.shtml

The Jason Project
http://www.jasonproject.org/

National Geographic Society
http://www.nationalgeographic.com/seas/

Public Broadcasting System
http://www.pbs.org/wgbh/nova/abyss/

Science News for Kids
http://www.sciencenewsforkids.org/articles/20041110/Feature1.asp

University of Delaware: Mission to the Abyss
http://www.ocean.udel.edu/extreme2002/

Woods Hole Oceanographic Institution
http://www.whoi.edu/k-12/

Index